ISLANDS
of the WORLD

Llyfrgelloedd Caerdydd
www.caerdydd.gov.uk/llyfrgelloedd
Cardiff Libraries
www.cardiff.gov.uk/libraries

a Capstone company — publishers for children

Engage Literacy is published in the UK by Raintree.
Raintree is an imprint of Capstone Global Library Limited, a company incorporated in England and Wales having its registered office at 264 Banbury Road, Oxford, OX2 7DY – Registered company number: 6695582

www.raintree.co.uk

Editorial credits
Marissa Kirkman, editor; Charmaine Whitman, designer; Kelly Garvin, media researcher; Katy LaVigne, production specialist

Image credits
Getty Images/Marcel Mochet/Staff, 23 (top); Minden Pictures/Roberto Rinaldi/NPL, 28 (t); Image courtesy Jacques Descloitres, MODIS Land Rapid Response Team at NASA GSFC, we acknowledge the use of Rapid Response imagery from the Land, Atmosphere Near real-time Capability for EOS (LANCE) system operated by the NASA/GSFC/Earth Science Data and Inf, 16 (bottom); National Geographic Creative/ Jason Edwards, 8 (bottom left); Shutterstock: aaabbbccc, 10 (b), 11 (top right), Alberto Loyo, 3, alexilena, cover bottom, Andrea Izzotti, 32 (left), Anton Balazh, 5 (t), 15 (t), Balky79, 30 (t), BlueOrange Studio, 17 (t), Blue Planet Studio, 32 (right), Boyloso, 15 (b), Calin Stan, 5 (b), cdrw, 20, Darrin Henry, 14, Dennis van de Water, 11 (t), DyziO, 23 (b), Evgeny Gorodetsky, 24, Felix Mizioznikov, 25 (t), FloridaStock, 27 (t), frees, 29 (t), haveseen, cover (middle right), Helen Hotson, 12 (b), 21 (t), icarmen13, 9, J. Bicking, 26 (b), Kalamurzing, backcover, Ken Weinrich, 27 (bottom right), Kvitka Fabian, 25 (b), Lewis Liu, 18 (b), Ilona Ignatova, 13 (t), Mario Hagen, 30 (b), Maxger, 18 (t), Miraphoto, 21 (b), Mitchell Franklin, 27 (bl), NickKont, cover (tr), okili77, 12 (t), Oleksandr Molotkovych, 7 (b), Peter Hermes Furian, 16 (t), 22 (r), PetrJanJuracka, 8 (br), PhotoEd, 13 (b), Pierre-Yves Babylon, 10 (t), PSboom, 18 (t), Rainer Lesniewski, 22 (l), Ryan M. Bolton, 11 (b), SARAWUT KUNDEJ, cover (tl), Sophiebalanay18, 19 (tr), Steve Heap, 19 (tl), Tessa Palmer, 29 (b), totophotos, 4, Trent Townsend, 28 (b), Trevel9to5 Drone Footage, 1, Tsuguliev, 31, Vadim Petrakov, cover (middle left), Vladim Nefedoff, 7 (t), Yevgen Belich, 6, Volina, 8 (t), 26 (t), Zeljika, 17 (b)
Artistic elements: Shutterstock: Ladislav Krajca, RoyStudioEU

21 20 19 18 17
10 9 8 7 6 5 4 3 2 1
Printed and bound in China.

Islands of the World

ISBN: 978 1 4747 4691 5

CONTENTS

coral island

WHAT IS AN ISLAND?

Islands are pieces of land surrounded by a body of water. They are found in oceans all over the world. Some islands have formed only in the last few hundred years. But most islands were formed thousands or even millions of years ago. They come in many shapes, sizes and climates. They are home to different types of plants and animals. There are five types of islands. These include continental, oceanic and tidal islands. There are also *barrier* and *coral* islands.

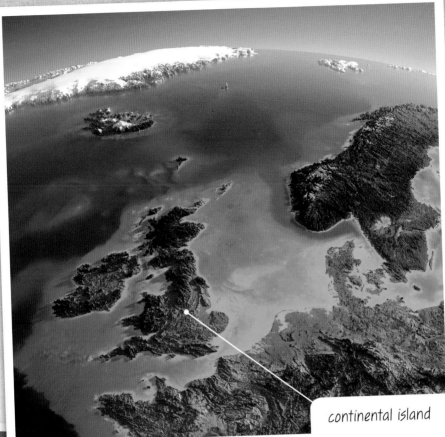

continental island

barrier island

5

Tasmania is a continental island off the coast of Australia.

CONTINENTAL ISLANDS

More continental islands
- Ireland
- New Zealand
- Tasmania
- Trinidad

Continental islands are islands that have separated from a larger body of land called a *continent*. There are seven continents in the world. Greenland is an island that was once part of North America, but is now separated by a narrow sea. Madagascar formed after breaking off from the continent of Asia, and Great Britain was once part of Europe. These islands are often the world's largest islands.

Greenland

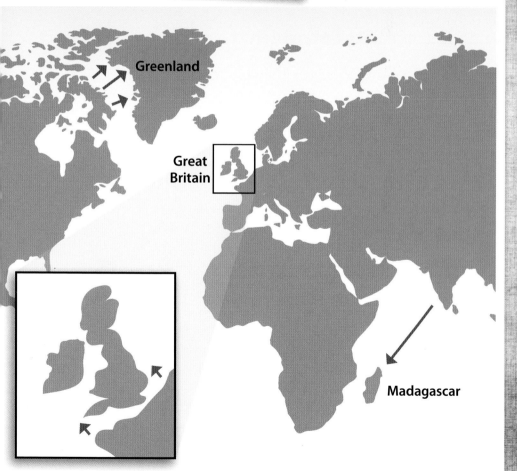

Greenland

Great Britain

Madagascar

Greenland

Greenland is located between the Arctic Ocean and the North Atlantic Ocean. It is the world's largest island in size. But only about 57,000 people live on it. That is because most of the island is covered in a sheet of ice.

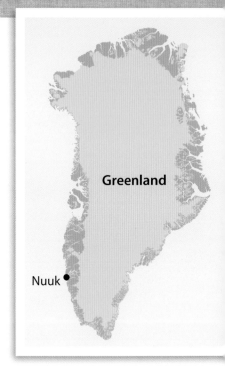

Greenland

Nuuk

Greenland also has very large pieces of ice and snow called *glaciers*. A few trees and patches of forest land dot the island, too.

ice sheet

glacier

Nuuk, Greenland

On the south-west coast of Greenland is the city of Nuuk. This city is home to the highest number of people in Greenland. The weather is very cold in the winter, but can warm up a bit in the summer. Seals, whales and fish make the oceans surrounding Greenland their home. Wildlife found on the island are foxes, polar bears and reindeer. People eat seafood and polar bear meat, which are some common foods on the island.

Fact: In Nuuk there are 21 hours of daylight in June and just 4 hours of daylight each day in December.

Madagascar

Madagascar is the fourth-largest island. It is located off the south-east coast of Africa in the Indian Ocean. Although it is smaller in size than Greenland, 25 million people live on this island.

Madagascar

There are mountains in the middle of the island.

rainforest

grassland

In the middle part of the island, there are volcanoes and high mountains. The east coast is covered with rainforests, and the west coast is mostly grassland. Beaches and palm trees surround the island. The weather here is hot and rainy in one season. It is cool and dry in the other season. People eat beef, chicken and lamb. They also eat rice and noodles, among other foods. Most of the animals on this island, such as the lemur, cannot be found in any other part of the world.

Fact: Madagascar is the oldest island in the world. It split off from India more than 85 million years ago.

Great Britain

Great Britain is the eighth-largest island in the world. It broke away from the continent of Europe about 9,000 years ago. The land across Great Britain is very mixed.

There are mountains in some areas and flat marshes in others.

This island is made up of the countries of England, Wales and Scotland. Together, Great Britain and Northern Ireland make up the United Kingdom.

marsh

London

London is the largest city on the island of Great Britain. The temperature is warm in the summer and cold in the winter. In England, it can rain throughout the year. Winters in Scotland can have strong winds, heavy rain and snow. Common foods from Great Britain are fish and chips, pies with meat and vegetables

fish and chips

and sweet scones. Wildlife includes different types of deer, foxes and badgers.

Fact: The highest point of Great Britain is the top of the Ben Nevis mountain in Scotland.

St Helena is an oceanic island in the South Atlantic Ocean.

OCEANIC ISLANDS

More oceanic islands
- Aleutian Islands
- Canary Islands
- Iceland
- Japan
- St Helena

Oceanic islands are not connected to a continent. Most of these islands form when volcanoes erupt on the ocean floor. The *lava* begins to pile up as it cools down. Over time it appears above water to form an island. The Galapagos Islands and the Hawaiian Islands are oceanic islands.

Japan is a country that is also an oceanic island.

Iceland is an oceanic island in the Atlantic Ocean.

Galapagos Islands, Ecuador

Galapagos Islands

SOUTH
AMERICA

The Galapagos Islands are made up of 13 main islands and 6 smaller islands. They form an *archipelago*, which is a group of islands spaced closely together. The islands are in the Pacific Ocean off the western coast of South America. The oldest islands are about 4 million years old. New islands are still forming.

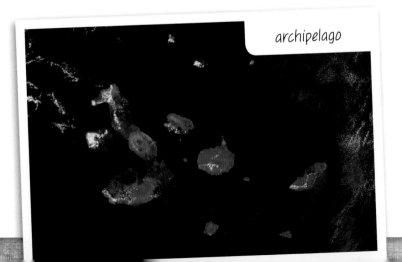

archipelago

prickly pear cactus

Today there are about 25,000 people who live on 4 of the Galapagos Islands. They have the warmest temperatures between December and May. The cool season is from June to November. Many people eat seafood that is caught nearby. Each day a boat brings fresh fruit, meat and water for the people on the islands to eat. Many special animals live on these islands, such as sea lions, crabs and giant tortoises. There are also many different types of plants, such as the lava cactus and the prickly pear cactus.

Fact: Galapagos tortoises can reach 1.5 metres long and weigh 226 kilograms. Some live to be 100 years old.

Galapagos tortoise

Hawaiian Islands, United States

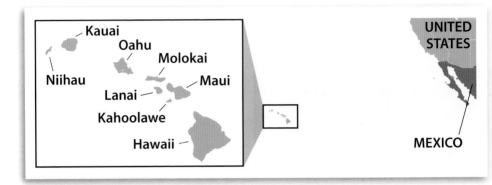

The Hawaiian Islands are made up of eight main islands and many other smaller islands in the Pacific Ocean. They are also an archipelago. Hawaii, also called the "Big Island", is the largest island. The island of Oahu has the most people at 953,207, and Hawaii has the second-largest number of people at 186,738. The temperature is warm in both the summer and in the winter.

Oahu

Hawaiian monk seal

The Hawaiian goose is the state bird.

People usually take short flights to travel between the islands, but there are also a few boats. On the islands people enjoy seafood, kalua pig (roasted pork) and pineapple, among other foods. There are many special birds and animals living here, such as the Hawaiian goose and the Hawaiian monk seal. Whales and dolphins also travel here each winter.

Fact: Kilauea is one of five volcanoes that form the "Big Island". It has been active since 1983.

Enoshima is a tidal island in the country of Japan.

TIDAL ISLANDS

Tidal islands are connected to a mainland by a strip of land that can only be seen during a low *tide*. This is when the sea has fallen to its lowest point. When the sea rises during a high tide, it completely covers the strip of land. One example of a tidal island is Mont Saint-Michel in Normandy, France.

More tidal islands

- Enoshima, Fujisawa, Japan
- Haji Ali Dargah, Mumbai, India
- St Michael's Mount, Cornwall, UK

The water level is low during low tide at St Michael's Mount.

The water level rises to cover the road during high tide at St Michael's Mount.

Mont Saint-Michel, Normandy, France

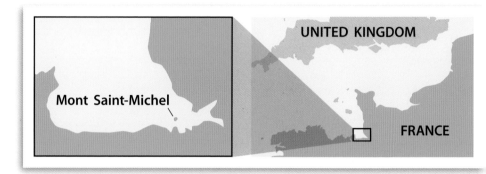

Mont Saint-Michel is a rocky tidal island near the north-west coast of France. People can get to the island by foot, horse-drawn carriage or shuttle bus. The tides rise and fall twice every 24 hours. When the high tide rises, it surrounds the island with water. Sometimes, the high tide covers all the roads leading to the island.

Millions of people visit this small island each year. But only about 40 people live on the island. The temperature on the island is warm in the summer and colder in the winter. Some common foods that people eat are seafood, lamb and a type of thin pancake called a crepe. Birds are the most common wildlife on the island.

Mont Saint-Michel

horse-drawn carriage

Great Barrier Island is a barrier island in New Zealand.

BARRIER ISLANDS

Barrier islands are made up of sand. They look like a strip of land running parallel to the mainland. They help to block heavy winds and waves from reaching the mainland. Between the barrier island and the mainland is often a calm body of water called a *lagoon*. These islands can change often because of strong wind, waves and storms. One example of this type of island is Hatteras Island in the US state of North Carolina.

More barrier islands

- Florida Keys, Florida, USA
- Great Barrier Island, New Zealand
- Long Island, New York, USA

The Florida Keys are barrier islands in the US state of Florida.

lagoon

Hatteras Island, North Carolina, United States

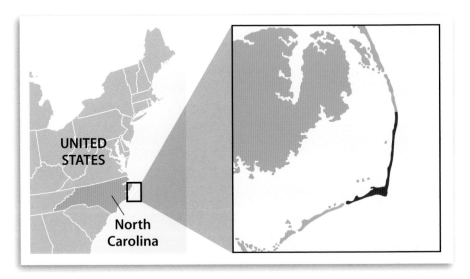

Hatteras Island lies parallel to the North Carolina coast in the Atlantic Ocean. It is connected to the mainland by bridges, and most people drive to the island. Another option is to take a ferry boat to the island.

ferry boat

Hatteras Island

There are about 3,500 people who live on the island year-round. More than 3 million people visit the island every year. Most people visit during the summer. The temperature is usually warmer in the summer and colder in the winter. Many people eat seafood, such as crabs and clams that they catch along the coast of the island. Sea turtles, lizards and even seals can be found on the island in the winter and spring.

clams

crabs

Heron Island

More coral islands

- The Bahama Islands
- Maldives

CORAL ISLANDS

Corals are the hard, shell-like skeletons of hundreds of tiny sea creatures. They come in several colours. When the hard shells join together in warm bodies of water, they create a type of land called a *coral reef*. Over time the coral reef can grow to form a large piece of land above water, called a coral island. One example of a coral island is Heron Island.

coral

Heron Island, Great Barrier Reef, Australia

Heron Island is in the Coral Sea at the end of the Great Barrier Reef. It is a national park that people can visit. White sandy beaches surround the island. Temperatures are fairly warm year-round. The island gets its name from the herons, a type of bird, which are a common part of island life. The island is also a nesting location for turtles. Each year, for 4 months, about 90 turtles can be found digging out holes in the sand to lay their eggs.

heron

ISLAND LIFE

There are different types of islands that come in many sizes, shapes and climates. There are also ways they are alike. Each of the five types of islands were formed in natural ways. They all have plants and some type of animal or sea creature living on or around them. They also have people who live or visit there.

one of the Palm Islands

Fact: One other island type, *artificial* islands, are made by people. The Palm Islands in Dubai are being made with sand from the sea floor and 7 million tonnes of mountain rock.

GLOSSARY

archipelago   group of islands spaced closely together

artificial   made by people

barrier   object that prevents access to something. A barrier island blocks damaging wind and waves from storms from reaching the mainland.

continent   one of Earth's seven large landmasses

corals   hard, sharp structures made up of the skeletons of millions of tiny creatures

coral reef   type of land made up of the hardened bodies of corals

glacier   large, slow-moving sheet of ice

island   piece of land that is smaller than a continent and is completely surrounded by water

lagoon   calm body of water between a barrier island and the mainland

lava   hot, liquid rock that pours out of a volcano when it erupts

tide   rising and falling of the ocean up and down the shore. There are usually two high tides and two low tides in one day.

INDEX